WASH & BRUSH UP

Eleanor Allen

Adam & Charles Black   London

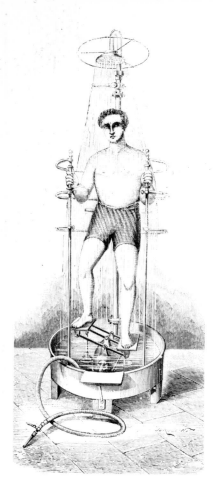

An ingenious Victorian shower,
to keep you fit as well as clean

Black's Junior Reference Books

General editor: R J Unstead

Published by A & C Black (Publishers) Ltd, 35 Bedford Row, London
WC1R 4JH

ISBN 0-7136-1639-3

First published 1976   Reprinted 1977, 1984

Filmset and printed in Great Britain by
BAS Printers Limited, Over Wallop, Hampshire

Contents

Hanging baths, used to punish lazy people during the middle ages—or so one writer said

A cart spraying water to lay the dust; Brixton, London, 1873

Pumping water by hand

Acknowledgements

The author and publishers are grateful to the following for permission to reproduce illustrations:
Armitage Shanks Ltd 16;
Birmingham Public Libraries 45;
Trustees of the British Museum 6, 40, 47, 51;
Crown Copyright, reproduced by permission of the Department of the Environment 7;
Edinburgh City Libraries 13, 51;
Mansell Collection 9, 10, 15, 19, 23, 28, 35, 38, 39, 40, 43, 50, 55, 62, 63;
Mary Evans Picture Library 1, 2, 15, 17, 18, 22, 23, 26, 30, 32, 38, 41, 42, 43, 45, 46, 48, 49, 52, 53, 54, 55, 57, 58, 59, 60;
Ian Moir 14;
National Portrait Gallery 27, 41, 52;
Radio Times Hulton Picture Library 3, 4, 5, 7, 8, 11, 12, 17, 18, 19, 21, 24, 27, 29, 30, 31, 32, 33, 34, 36, 37, 41, 54, 56, 60, 61, 63;
Science Museum 11, 16, 33, 57, 58, 61, 62;
Master and Fellows of Trinity College, Cambridge 20;
Unilever Educational Publications 24;
York Archaeological Trust 6.

How clean is clean?

If you were to find yourself transported back through time to a street in medieval, Elizabethan, or even early Victorian times on a hot summer's day, you would find the smell unbearable.

The street itself would stink—of sewage, dung and rotting refuse, and the people would stink too—of stale unwashed clothes, sweaty unwashed bodies, and foul breath. You would probably turn up your sensitive modern nose and stare appalled at the dirt around you, wondering how people could bear to live like that.

But you would be judging them by the standards of this present age, and this is an age which pays great attention to cleanliness. We can afford to. For the majority of us in this country today keeping clean is easy. We have a constant supply of clean water at the turn of a tap, soap at a price within everyone's reach, lavatories that flush away sewage, and machines that wash our clothes.

Before dismissing our ancestors as filthy, insanitary creatures who cared nothing for cleanliness, we must remember that they had none of these things.

A medieval lady empties her slops out of the window

In a Victorian slum. You can see the outdoor privy on the left, the tin wash tub and the washing hung to dry over an open drain

Early bronze bucket

A Roman sewer in York, large
enough to stand up in

Water supply and sanitation

The Romans

Early man had no difficulty in supplying himself with
sufficient water for all his needs, for he always lived
near a river, spring or lake. Sanitation (getting rid of
sewage) presented no problems for him either, for
villages were small and surrounded by open country-
side. It was only when men began to live together in
large groups that problems of water supply and sanitation arose.

When the Romans arrived in Britain they began to
build towns. It was not so easy for town dwellers to
go down to the nearest river or stream for water so
the Romans dug wells, provided public fountains,
and even piped in water to fill the public baths.

Each Roman town dealt with the problem of sewage
in its own way. Lincoln had an underground sewerage
system where every street had its own drain and
houses were linked to it. But in most towns sewage
was thrown with other rubbish into a gutter in the
street or buried in pits.

Beaumaris Castle, built by Edward I, had a fine moat into which the sewage would have drained

Castles

When the Normans built castles, they too had to provide for large numbers of people living together in one place.

Sometimes, if enemies laid siege to a castle, it was impossible for anyone to leave it for weeks, so a good water supply was essential. This came from a well in the basement, usually fitted with a windlass and bucket for drawing it up.

Lavatories, known as 'garderobes' were built inside the thick walls. They were small dark rooms containing nothing more than a draughty stone shaft, down which the sewage fell into a pit in the foundations or, in later times, into the moat. In hot weather the smell from the moat was vile and conditions inside castles could become bad enough during a long siege to cause the defenders to surrender. This happened at Rochester in 1088.

Streams and rivers as well as moats acted as open sewers. Manor houses and other buildings which stood near a river or stream usually arranged to drain their sewage into it and monasteries built their 'necessariums' where they could either drain into a stream or even be flushed out by it.

In Carisbrooke Castle, a donkey was used to turn the windlass to raise water from the well

Collecting water from a well

Ancient water pipes made from elm trunks were dug up in London about 40 years ago. Such pipes were first used about 1600

Medieval towns

In the Middle Ages, as towns grew larger, the problems of supplying their populations with water and disposing of their sewage increased.

The problem was particularly great in London. From about AD1280 conduits (water tunnels) were built to carry water into the city. It was delivered at fountains where it could be drawn off and carried away in buckets. There were also wells from which the water was pumped by hand pumps.

Every drop of household water had to be carried home in buckets through the busy streets. The poor had to do the job themselves, but those who could afford it paid a water-carrier to deliver the water for them.

There was no system of underground sewers as there is today and people had only buckets for lavatories. Many people built cesspits in their gardens and emptied the buckets into those. Due to lack of space, the cesspits were often only a few paces from the house and from the neighbouring garden.

Burying victims of the plague

The old English word for lavatory was 'gong'. The men who were employed from time to time to empty the cesspits were called 'gong fermors'. Their job was so loathsome that they were paid three times as much as ordinary unskilled workers.

People who had no cesspit threw their sewage outside the door or into the wide, open drain that ran down the centre of the street. It was a very nasty and un-healthy thing to do, but there was often nowhere else to put it. Occasionally carts came to carry it away to dung heaps, called 'laystows', on waste ground out-side the town, or tip it into a nearby river.

Piles of sewage and other rotting refuse caused a vile stench in the narrow streets. But worse still, this filth was a breeding ground for germs and for rats and flies which spread the germs. When the weather was hot the germs multiplied and there were outbreaks of plague and other diseases.

People did not realise that the dirt bred germs which caused disease. They did not know that when they tipped the sewage into the rivers they were spreading the germs to their water supply. They believed that disease was caused by the stench (miasma) the dirt gave off.

A doctor holds a pomander to his nose, believing that it will protect him from the plague

Ornate pomanders for holding herbs and perfumes. Sometimes people simply used a dried orange stuck with cloves

When people walked through the streets they often clutched a sprig of herbs to their noses. They thought that a pleasant smell would protect their nostrils from the stench which could cause disease.

Because of the state of the streets it was impossible to open the windows of town houses. Rooms became smelly and musty. People tried to disguise the smell by strewing sweet-smelling herbs such as lavender, sage or thyme over the floor, or burning sweet-smelling woods such as juniper or cypress. Sometimes they made pot-pourris out of herbs and flowers or puffed perfumed powder into the air from a pomander made of skin. Even so, the sickly smell of sewage must have lingered.

Elizabethan times

Despite all the show and splendour of this age, water supplies and sanitation remained as primitive as they had been in medieval times. Water was still collected in buckets from fountains and wells; sewage was still tipped into the street, despite regulations against it.

But there was at least one person who thought about improving the sanitary arrangements. He was Sir John Harington, godson of Queen Elizabeth. In 1596 he designed a water closet which would flush away sewage into a drain.

He had the model constructed in his house near Bath, and it is said that Elizabeth had one installed in Richmond Palace. But most people thought the invention was a joke and it never came into common use. Apart from the difficulties of supplying enough water to flush it, the Elizabethans did not have the technical skill needed to lay the great length of drainage pipes they would have needed for large numbers of closets.

People did not, in fact, start to have waterclosets installed until nearly 200 years later. In the meantime, throughout the 17th, 18th and much of the 19th centuries, they kept to primitive methods.

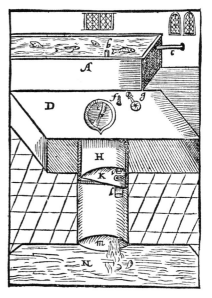

Harington's water closet. The seat cover was meant to be a scallop shell

An old conduit, where townspeople came for water. 'Conduit' meant a fountain as well as a water pipe

Chamber pots, buckets and close-stools

Bedrooms were equipped with chamber pots which were either pushed discreetly out of sight underneath the bed, or stored in a small cupboard. The presence of a pot in the same room in which people slept left a sickening smell in the bed fabrics and furniture, as this Victorian writer points out:

> 'the bedrooms smell of human exudations. This is especially so in inns . . . coming to the great capital, as a rule you cannot get a bed to rest on without nausea . . .'

But despite this drawback, chamber pots continued to be part of the standard equipment of many homes until quite recent times. They were usually bought as part of a toilet set consisting of chamber pot, water basin and jug. The common sort were earthenware, but in the 17th and 18th centuries the rich went to the extravagance of having them made out of pewter, or even silver. In all households emptying out the chamber pots was one of the servants' tasks.

'The Emperor'—a magnificent shiny silver chamber pot which once belonged to Napoleon's brother

In larger houses there was sometimes a special room containing buckets for use during the day as a lavatory. But it was small, without windows or ventilation and must have been very unpleasant.

Some richer folk used commodes known as 'close-stools', made with comfortable, though unhygienic padded seats. Some of the close-stools made for royalty were very elaborate and had seats padded with velvet. They seem to have been kept in almost any room in the house. Samuel Pepys, who kept a diary in the reign of Charles II, thought his such a fine item of furniture that he kept it in his sitting room!

Whatever sort of container was used, the contents were disposed of in the same primitive ways. There were still no really effective sewerage systems. In many towns people continued to empty their slops into the gutters.

Even in 1905, rubbish and slops were thrown into a gutter in the street in this Scottish town of Newhaven

Early 20th century sewage collectors

For a Pot-pourri

Take three parts of a basin of rose petals, dried in an airy room away from strong sunlight, and add a cupful of dried thyme, lavender and rosemary, together with the dried and powdered skin of an orange and some cloves.

Mix well together and place in a pot-pourri bowl made of decorated wood or china—lid pierced with a number of large holes through which the perfume escapes.

London after the Great Plague filled in the open gutters and insisted that people should either bury their rubbish or put it out in buckets for collection, but other places were slow to follow suit. As late as 1808 the inhabitants of Exeter were still emptying their sewage into the gutters.

Better-off folk still had their own cesspits. In towns they were now often situated in the cellar of the house, directly underneath the living quarters. They were emptied so infrequently that sometimes they overflowed into the neighbouring cellar.

As late as 1844 no fewer than 53 overflowing cesspits were found beneath Windsor Castle. These cesspits were dangerous sources of infection and households frequently suffered from mysterious attacks of sore throat, diarrhoea, or even worse ailments.

In these large, wealthy households just as much as in poorer ones it was difficult to escape the smell of sewage. Housewives still did their best to disguise it, by burning small cakes of fragrant gum resin in china perfume burners, lighting perfumed candles for special occasions, and putting out bowls of pot-pourri.

Boghouses and water pipes

Throughout the 18th and much of the 19th century it became common practice for people to have a privy or boghouse in the back yard, or at the bottom of the garden for use during the day. It consisted of a small hut with, inside, a wooden seat constructed over a pit into which the sewage fell.

Occasionally 'night soil men' came and emptied the pit with buckets, but often the sewage was allowed to seep away into the surrounding earth. If there was a well nearby, its water was contaminated.

Wells and rivers were still the chief sources of water supply and most were contaminated by sewage. Carts still tipped their loads into the rivers and any drains that existed discharged into them.

During the 17th and 18th centuries some wealthy households started to have water piped into cisterns in their houses. From the cistern it was pumped to a tap in the kitchen. But they received supplies only two or three times a week and the private companies who performed the service charged a very high price. Ordinary folk still collected their water by the bucket.

London's 'night soil men'

Above: an earth closet. This was placed over a hole in the ground. A layer of earth was shaken over the sewage.

Left: a privy tacked onto the back of a house

Some lavatory bowls were handsomely decorated

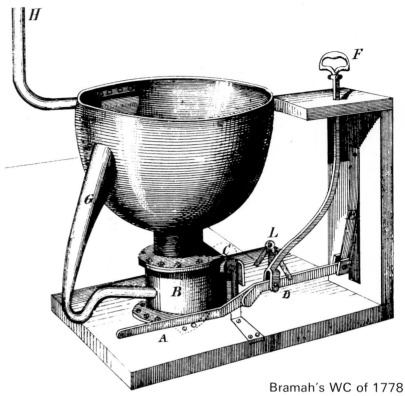

Bramah's WC of 1778

Water closets

In the mid 1770s Alexander Cumming invented a new type of water closet which a few rich people who could afford piped water and drains began to fit inside their houses. The closet was flushed by water from an overhead cistern, but the special feature was its 'stink trap'. About a foot below the pan the soil pipe was bent into an **S** shape which was kept filled with water—a design we still use today. This was supposed to seal off the smell from the drain. Unfortunately the closet's mechanism was not efficient. The bend tended to become congested with sewage and foul gases were given off.

An improved version was developed by Joseph Bramah in 1778, but it still continued to give off foul gases. Because it was usually placed in a small, un-ventilated room under the stairs, it often had a worse effect on people's health than the old methods.

Gradually better water closets were devised, but it was not until the 1870s that they became really efficient.

Ornate lion WC

The need for progress

In the early 19th century the populations of Britain's towns expanded very rapidly. Soon the old methods of supplying water and disposing of sewage, which had been inadequate even for smaller numbers, became completely incapable of coping with the problem.

Poorer people lived herded together in filthy tenements, clustered round courtyards flowing with open cesspools. There was so much extra sewage that there were not enough night soil men to deal with it and dung heaps piled up.

The water was turned on for perhaps only a couple of hours a day and people had to queue at the standpipes and wells for their water or do without. The water was so contaminated it had to be allowed to stand for several hours to allow the sediment to settle.

Half of London's population had its water from a stretch of the Thames into which 200 underground drains discharged. Under these conditions it is not surprising that around the middle of the century the country was swept by epidemics of cholera, typhus and smallpox from which thousands died.

Grim living conditions in a London slum: a privy in the back yard and a rain barrel served each overcrowded house

Queuing for water at a stand-pipe

Privies in Bermondsey, in the East end of London. The sewage dropped straight into the water supply

Constructing a large new London sewer

Local authorities began to look closely at methods of improving water supplies and sanitation, and local boards of health were set up. One of the first moves was to take water supplies, drainage, sewerage and cleansing out of the hands of private companies and make them the responsibility of town councils.

Then the authorities began to plan the necessary improvements. It took a great deal of time. Dozens of reservoirs, hundreds of kilometres of sewer and water pipes and thousands of closets and wash basins were needed. Building and constructing them took many years.

In the 1890s Dr Alfred Salter of Bermondsey reported a case where there was still only one water closet for 25 houses. Every morning men, women and children had to queue up outside it before going to work or school.

When private water closets were built for poorer homes they were usually draughty, uncomfortable places built in a line at the end of a back yard or next to the back porch. It was not until after the Second World War that an indoor water closet became common in poorer homes. But even today not everybody has one. There are a few people even now in country areas who still use a bucket as their ancestors did and bury the contents in the garden.

Washing and bathing

The Romans

Early man probably bathed in the rivers or lakes sometimes, but the first people to introduce regular bathing into Britain, with special facilities for it, were the Romans. The Romans had public baths in their towns and private ones on a smaller scale in their villas.

Bathing in Roman times was a leisurely process. When a Roman visited a bath-house he was greeted by a slave who led him to a changing room to undress. Then he went into a tepid room and bathed.

After bathing he went into a hot room which made him sweat (like a modern Turkish bath). He sat on a bench and perhaps chatted to his friends there. Next he entered a massage room where slaves rubbed his body with oil, and toned up his skin with a scraper called a 'strigil'. Finally, before going out again into the open air, he might plunge into a cold bath to close his pores.

Heat for the different rooms was provided by a 'hypocaust' system. The floors of the bath-house were raised on small pillars and heat from furnaces stoked up by slaves circulated underneath them and up the cavity walls.

Roman washing equipment, including strigils and oil flasks

Remains of the luxurious Roman bath-house in Bath

Monasteries

Ordinary people do not seem to have cared much about washing themselves after the departure of the Romans. Monasteries, however, made rules about washing and bathing which monks had to obey.

Near the refectory where the monks ate their meals the monastery provided a 'laver', which was a stone trough containing cold water. There the monks were expected to wash their hands before and after each meal. Hand washing was considered essential because forks were not used and they ate with their fingers.

Monasteries also contained a bath-house, equipped with wooden tubs and clean hay for bath-mats. The monks were allowed to have warm water for bathing up to four times a year.

A medieval plan showing the water pipes of the monastery at Canterbury. Water was piped from a nearby lake. The necessarium contained the monks' latrines

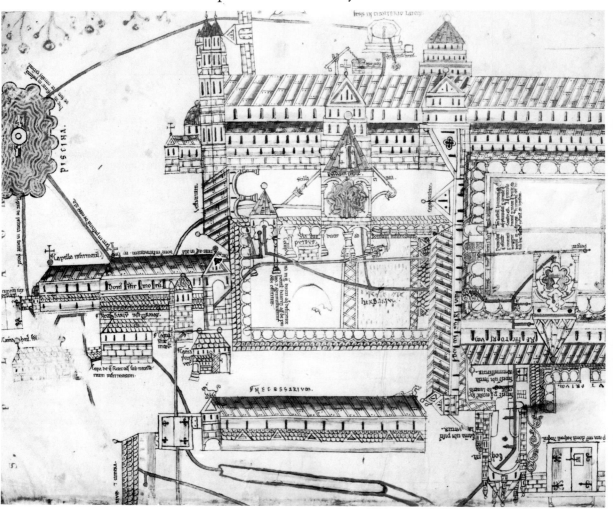

A communal bath was a pleasant social occasion, with music, food and drink

Communal bathing in Norman times

By Norman times it had become fashionable for wealthy families to enjoy a hot bath occasionally. They bathed in large round wooden tubs, filled with water which the servants had heated in pots over the fire.

Heating enough water to fill a large tub was such hard work that, when a bath had been prepared, the Normans made the most of it.

Sometimes a whole family and their guests bathed together while the water was hot. That idea seems rather startling to us these days, but the Normans had different standards from ours. To them it was a sensible idea and not at all improper.

In castles and manor houses it was the custom for people to wash their hands at the table in a small bowl. A servant or a page carried a jug of water, called an 'aquamanile', from guest to guest, trickling the water over their hands and offering a napkin to dry them on.

Young girls tending a guest in his bath: massaging him, heating his water and bringing him a garland of flowers and a drink

Men in a public bath-house, talking, drinking and listening to music

An Aromatic Bath

In a sufficient quantity of river water, boil, for the space of two or three minutes, one or more of the following aromatic herbs: clove; July-flowers; balm; sweet basil; rosemary; wild thyme; wild mint; or any other herbs that have an agreeable scent.

Having strained off the liquor from the herbs, add to a little brandy or camphorated spirits of wine.

This is said to be an excellent bath to strengthen the limbs; it removes pain, the consequence of cold and promotes perspiration.

The 'stews' of the Middle Ages

In the Middle Ages public bath-houses were reintroduced into England. They provided steam baths like those of the Romans, though not so luxurious. The idea was brought from Turkey by the Crusaders.

Bath-houses, quickly nicknamed 'stews', were set up in larger towns and the townsfolk seem to have used them fairly regularly. But unfortunately the baths needed so much wood for heating the water that forests near to towns were rapidly used up and supplies dwindled. Also it was found that these bath-houses caused the spread of infection. Gradually they fell into disuse.

Wealthy families kept a ewer and a basin of pewter in their bedrooms for washing their hands and faces. At meal times they continued to pass a bowl of water round the table for washing hands, though a book on manners which was written at the time found it necessary to warn men not to spit in it.

These well-to-do households used soap. There were recipes for making it at home by boiling up animal fat with wood ash, but from the 14th century onwards it was possible to buy soap which had been made commercially in England. The most important area for soap-making at that time was around Bristol. This early soap was dark in colour and rather unattractive in appearance. Finer soaps were imported from Spain, the most famous from Castile.

Rich lady getting out of her bath

Men and women sometimes bathed together

Above: Tudor cake of soap

Below: Soap and candle factory, about 1830

Elizabethan times

Soap-making was growing in importance as a trade in Elizabeth's reign, though scented soap of good quality was still a luxury. The trade had spread to London and we hear of soap being made at various places in or around the city, such as Bankside near Blackfriars.

But despite the growth in soap-making, the Elizabethan age was not noted for its cleanliness.

Even Elizabeth herself, who had bathrooms installed at Windsor Castle, only took a bath once a month 'whether she required it or not'! Her subjects must have thought it was necessary to bath far less frequently.

Another famous woman of the time, Mary Queen of Scots, occasionally bathed in wine—not in order to keep clean, but because she believed it would preserve her good looks.

Queen Elizabeth I. Her elaborate gown could never be washed

An Excellent Perfume for Gloves

Take Ambergris a drachm, the same quantity of Civet, mix these ingredients well, and rub into the gloves with fine cotton wool, and so press the perfume into them.

To disguise the smell of their unwashed bodies, the Elizabethans (both men and women) sprinkled themselves lavishly with perfumes such as musk, ambergris and civet. As well as scenting themselves and their clothes, they also scented their fans and leather objects. Elizabeth was particularly fond of perfumed leather gloves and owned a cloak of perfumed leather.

Large houses had a 'still room' where perfumed waters were made from flowers and herbs, using recipes handed down from generation to generation. The most common was rose water which was sprinkled over the body, hands and hair.

A servant brings a jug of
water and a basin for the lady
to wash her hands

Demi Bain de Vapeurs.
Half dampend Bad.

Taking a steam bath, from the
waist downwards

Hummums

Public baths returned to fashion again in the late 17th
century. Travellers who had visited the Near East
returned with tales of Turkish public baths, as the
Crusaders had done. They called the baths by their
Persian name, Hummums, but nicknamed them
'hothouses'.

Only wealthier people seem to have visited them and
their visits were not frequent. Samuel Pepys noted
one day in his diary that his wife had gone to a hot-
house to bath herself. When she returned she made a
resolution that she would keep herself very clean in
future, but Pepys strongly doubted it. His doubts
seem to have been correct. Though he kept his diary
for nine years, it is the only time that he mentions his
wife having a bath!

Private bathrooms in houses in the late 17th and early
18th centuries were very rare indeed. When the Duke
of Devonshire had a blue and white marble bathroom
installed at Chatsworth in Derbyshire in 1694, it was
considered quite a wonder.

Georgian times

Bathrooms continued to be rare throughout the 18th century. Well-to-do people who wanted to wash usually did so in their bedrooms at a washstand on which stood a bowl and a ewer of water. If they took an occasional bath it was in a tin bath in front of the bedroom fire. Servants had to fetch water for the bath from the pump outside, heat it over the kitchen fire, and then carry it upstairs.

Poorer people who had no servants to fetch and carry water for them and no time to collect it for them-selves, went dirty. Grimy faces, and hands ingrained with dirt must have been a common sight. Even a great lady called Lady Mary Wortley Montague does not seem to have been at all embarrassed when a French woman commented on the grubby state of her hands. Her frank reply was, 'Ah, madame, if you were to see my feet!'

The high cost of soap put it out of the reach of ordi-nary folk. It was heavily taxed from the 17th century onwards and its manufacture was strictly controlled. At times the tax was as high as the cost of the soap itself. Soap-boiling pans were fitted with lids and each evening excise men went round closing and locking them so that soap-makers could not cheat by making extra soap secretly at night. Many people con-tinued to make their own soap at home, sometimes scenting it with herbs.

Lady Mary Wortley Montague

Washstands

The baths in Bath, drawn in 1672

Crowded rooms, particularly at balls, reeked with sweaty, unwashed bodies. Both men and women still perfumed themselves strongly with civet and musk, but at times the atmosphere became unbearable. For such occasions ladies had rings made with a little hinged box containing a few grains of scented powder which they could surreptitiously inhale.

Some people suspected that frequent bathing was not good for the health. A famous writer of the 18th century, called Dr Johnson, shook his head with grave disapproval when he was shown a bathroom a friend had installed in his home. 'Let well alone and be content,' Johnson advised. 'I hate immersion.'

But not everyone shared Dr Johnson's views on 'immersion'. Spas such as Bath were becoming popular with people who thought that sitting up to the neck in the warm mineral waters would cure all sorts of illness. Also, in the second half of the 18th century, bathing in the sea became fashionable—the colder it was, the healthier.

Bags to Scent Linen

Take Rose Leaves dried in the shade, Cloves beat to a gross powder, and Mace scraped. Mix them together, and fill little bags with this composition.

Early nineteenth century

One man in particular in this age strongly believed in the importance of personal cleanliness. He was a fashionable friend of the Prince Regent called 'Beau' Brummell.

It is said that he spent two hours a day bathing in water and milk, a habit which astonished many people. But Brummell had a great deal of influence over the rich young men of his day. They copied his clothes, his manners, and even started to copy his ideas on cleanliness. It soon became the height of fashion among the rich to be scrupulously clean.

Brummell also said that no gentleman should ever use perfume, but his influence was not so great on this point. Toilet waters such as Eau de Cologne were popular with both sexes, but particularly with men.

It became the fashion to carry around a container made of gold or silver, called a vinaigrette, which held a fine sponge soaked in aromatic vinegar. There was also a ring for the ladies called a fountain ring, which released a fine spray of their favourite perfume a foot into the air when they pressed it. In 1822 the king, George IV, spent £263 on perfume—as much as ten farm labourers' wages for a year.

Bottle for sprinkling rose water

The fastidious Beau Brummell

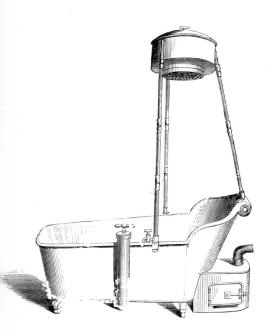

Bath with shower

Victoria's reign

Bathrooms were still so rare that when Victoria became Queen in 1837, there were still none installed at Buckingham Palace.

Baths were taken, if at all, in a tin bath called a hip bath in front of the bedroom fire. Heating and carrying the water remained drudgery for the servants.

In the early years of the reign some adventurous middle-class families tried to overcome the difficulties by doing without hot water and bathing in the kitchen. They sat in a tin bath full of cold water with perhaps just a canful of hot poured in to take the chill off. They consoled themselves with the belief that cold water was better for their health than hot.

Really up-to-date families experimented with a primitive sort of shower arrangement which sent a hail of icy water through a bucket pierced with holes.

Servants had to bring jugs of water for the bath

Keeping clean was a terrible struggle for the poor, who often had to cook, wash and live in one room

Gradually, middle-class Victorians began to make a virtue of being clean. They believed in the saying 'cleanliness is next to godliness' and they looked down with horror on the lower classes, referring to them as 'the great unwashed'.

But the fact that they were 'unwashed' was no fault of the poorer families. They simply had not the means to be clean. Think of the problems—one cold water tap often shared by ten or twelve families and the water turned on only two hours a day; perhaps nothing to collect the water in except a basin; no private place in which to wash when as many as six or eight people might be sharing two rooms; soap taxed so highly they could not afford to buy it.

In 1842 the Liverpool authorities decided to bring back the idea of public bath-houses, which would provide the poor with the facilities they lacked at home. Other authorities copied the idea and it proved a success, though of course not everybody used the baths.

Early Victorian public bath-house

Many Victorian mothers sewed their children into a special item of clothing like a vest at the beginning of winter, to protect the children's chests. They did not unpick it again until spring, so throughout the winter neither the child nor the garment was washed. This practice continued into the twentieth century in some places.

An extraordinary steam bath

Victorian manufacturers began to experiment with new ways of making bathing simpler and pleasanter. They produced bath-tubs in all sorts of shapes. The hip bath was still the most popular, but there were also Sitz baths, square or oval with a little seat to sit on; lounge baths to lie in (sometimes disguised as couches); slipper baths in which one could submerge the whole body apart from the head; portable Turkish baths for use in the home; even 'tourists' baths' which could do double use as travelling trunks!

In the 1840s some richer families had a cold water supply laid on which they arranged to have piped and pumped upstairs into a bath-tub. This was usually set in a corner of the bedroom. Unfortunately the bath still had to be emptied by hand and the water, of course, was icy cold.

Inventors tried ways of heating the water after the bath had been filled. Some baths had gas burners underneath. The system worked, but the bather had to take care to turn the burners off before he got in, otherwise it was like stepping into a cooking pot. A better type of bath-water heater was invented in the 1860s. It had a tall boiler with a gas furnace underneath and was called a 'geyser'.

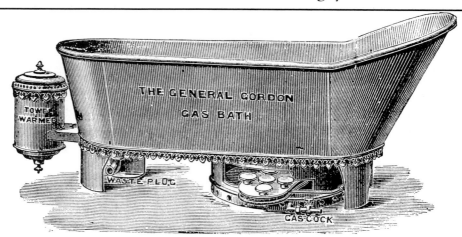

THE "GENERAL GORDON" GAS BATH.

This is a well made Bath, the sides being of best sheet Iron, tinned and japanned white inside, dark oak outside. The bottom being copper is a good conductor of heat, and is so little affected by the gas as to be much more durable than iron would be.

It is fitted with Waste Plug and loose Bent Union for attaching pipe, movable Towel Warmer, and powerful Atmospheric Burner. Price complete, including Gas Tap—

No. 1676. 5 feet .. .. £5 10 0 | No. 1677. 5 feet 6 inches .. £6 0 0

Spray and Plunge Bath.   Lavatory.   Dressing Table. Bidet.   W.C.

During the 1860s many families who had spare bed-rooms turned them into bathrooms by installing fixed bath-tubs. Hands and faces were still usually washed in bedrooms at marble-topped washstands, though by the 1880s manufacturers were turning out elaborate bathroom suites which included wash-basins.

Bath-tubs of the 1880s were being made of a new material—cast iron. The insides were painted, often in a marbled pattern. Painted tubs soon became shabby, however. Mr Pooter in a book called *The Diary of a Nobody* tried repainting his with some new 'Pink-ford's' red enamel paint. Unfortunately, after filling the tub with really hot water from the geyser, the paint dissolved and he stepped out 'perfectly red all over' and thought he had cut an artery and was bleeding to death.

Cast iron is still the usual material for bath-tubs today, but since about 1910 they have been coated with vitreous enamel, a substance which is far harder and more long-lasting than paint.

An elaborate bathroom suite

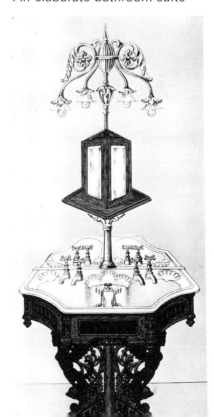

"I have found PEARS' SOAP matchless for the hands and complexion."

In 1853 the heavy tax on soap was removed, at last putting it within the price range of almost everyone. By the 1880s soap sales had increased so much that soap firms were running big advertising campaigns to attract the new buyers. Some adverts made very exaggerated claims.

By the end of the 19th century, bathrooms had become fairly common, even in ordinary homes, though they often contained only a bath and no wash-basin. Bathrooms in houses built before the Second World War were sometimes so narrow that there was scarcely space to stand.

Many smaller homes remained without bathrooms, however, either because there was nowhere to put them, or because owners or landlords would not bear the cost of having them installed. Some houses remain without bathrooms even today, and where large houses have been split up into flats, many households still have to share a bathroom.

Complexion

Nowadays we would not find a face attractive if there was a layer of dirt beneath the make-up. Nor would we find an elaborate hair-do attractive if we knew it was infested with lice. But in the past people were not always so particular. In their pursuit of the fashionable look of the age they often ignored cleanliness.

Face creams and lotions

Women have used face creams and lotions as substitutes for soap and water since Roman times. They have believed that these concoctions would not only clean their skin but would beautify it too.

In the Middle Ages women made herbal creams and other ointments at home using traditional recipes. Some of these recipes remained in use until the end of the 17th century. All sorts of odd ingredients went into them, such as dung, ass's milk and goat hair, as well as more obvious ones like herbs, flower petals, lemon juice, or cucumber water. In the reign of Charles II even puppy dog urine was recommended for improving the complexion and Samuel Pepys's wife was one of the brave ladies who tried it.

A Cosmetic Water, of great Use to prevent Pitts after the Small-Pox

Dissolve an ounce and an half of Salt in a pint of Mint-water; boil them together, and skim the liquor.

It is very useful to wash the face with after the Small-Pox, in order to clear away the scabs, allay the itching, and remove the redness.

Greek lady at her toilette

Doubtless some of the recipes worked and even the more unpleasant and unhygienic of them were not likely to do any great harm. But there were other face washes that were not so harmless. These were the ones made of mercury water which were popular with the rich in Elizabethan and Georgian times. If they were used frequently they ate into the flesh and left nasty scars.

Strangely enough, in Georgian times, whilst fashionable women were using these dangerous washes, they were shunning plain water as harmful. A book on etiquette advised its readers to wipe their faces every morning with a piece of white linen, but warned that washing in water made them too sensitive to cold and sunburn. Some ladies boasted that they had never washed their faces in their lives, for fear of spoiling their complexions.

A Water that gives a Gloss to the Skin

Take an handful of Bean, Elder, and Bugloss Flowers, a small Pidgeon clean drawn, the Juice of two lemons, four ounces of Salt, and five ounces of Camphor, distill them in a vapour bath; add to the distilled Water a few grains of Musk, and expose it to the sun for the space of a month, observing to take the vessel indoors every night.

The way to use this Water, is to dip a fine napkin in it, and gently rub the face therewith.

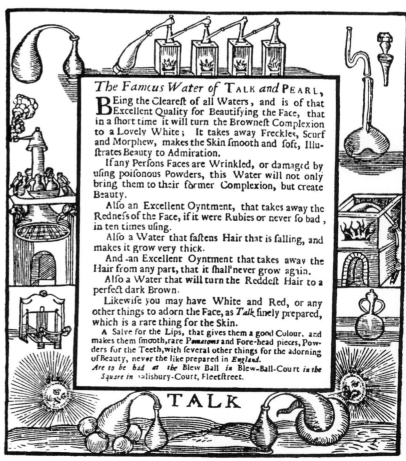

Advertisement for beauty preparations, in the time of Queen Anne

It was fashionable to wear patches of black taffeta on the face

Patching

But no matter what sort of lotions they smeared on to their faces, many people could never hope to have a good complexion if they had suffered from smallpox. This disease flourished in dirty conditions and attacked rich and poor alike, leaving their faces pitted and marked.

In the reign of Queen Anne it was common to see people wearing small patches of black taffeta to cover unsightly blemishes. Patching became the fashion even for those with nothing to hide. It was often carried to extremes, as this Frenchman pointed out:

> 'In England the young, old, handsome, ugly are all bepatched till they are bed-rid. I have counted fifteen patches or more, upon the Swarthy, wrinkled phiz of a Hag three-score and ten and upwards . . .'

Though patching might have hidden some of the blemishes, a smooth complexion could only be achieved by plastering on layers of make-up. Until the middle of the last century it was quite common for men as well as women to resort to make-up, particularly rouge.

Dusting the hair with powder

The finishing touches to the make-up

Ceruse

Throughout history from the time of the Romans, the colour of complexion most favoured by the English has been pink and white. In fashionable circles it was usually produced by make-up.

The height of the fashion was in Elizabethan and Georgian times when people used a dangerous whitener on their faces, called ceruse. It contained poisonous white lead. After using a mercury wash they coated their faces, necks, arms and bosoms with a thick layer of ceruse and rubbed a rouge called 'Spanish red' on to their cheeks. Sometimes they glazed over the make-up with egg white, giving it a hard, marbled finish.

If they used this make-up constantly they could begin to suffer the effects of lead poisoning—their skins dried up, their hair fell out and they developed dreadful stomach ailments. Some women even died. One such 'victim to cosmetics' was said to have been Maria Gunning, the beautiful Countess of Coventry, who died at the age of 27.

Although some men painted themselves with ceruse too, they do not seem to have been as badly affected by it as women, perhaps because they painted only their faces.

Victorian times and the present day

Make-up went out of fashion in Victorian times and none but the very daring used it. A fresh, childlike complexion was what women aimed to have. They still applied home-made face creams or bought preparations such as 'Beetham's Glycerine and Cucumber', but the Pears adverts persuaded them that soap and water could also be an aid to beauty.

In the 20th century make-up became not only fashionable again, but easier to obtain. Cosmetic firms began to make products which previously had to be concocted at home. These firms began to compete with each other through advertising to sell their bewildering varieties of toilet soaps, face creams, lotions and face packs.

Many advertisements played on people's uncertainty by referring to hidden dirt and impurities. They also suggested that no face could be attractive unless it was thoroughly clean and hinted that a thoroughly clean face must be attractive.

Nowadays cleanliness and attraction are so closely linked by advertising that some young girls and women are persuaded to buy cleansing creams and lotions in the hope that they will actually make them more beautiful.

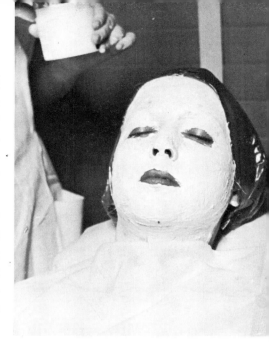

A face pack, used to cleanse the skin, 1930

Advertisement for face cream, 1913

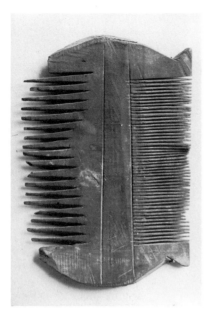

Roman double-sided wooden comb

Hair

Washing and rinsing one's hair uses up quite a lot of water, especially if it is long. Until homes began to have piped water it was as difficult for people to wash their hair as it was for them to have a bath.

Rich Romans with their excellent washing facilities found it easy to take good care of their hair. They used combs made of boxwood, ivory or tortoiseshell and had their servants dress it in elaborate styles with curling irons. Sometimes they used hair dyes or wore wigs. The men were usually clean shaven and paid frequent visits to barbers' shops or were shaved by their servants.

The Saxons too, though their general standards of cleanliness were low, seem to have given time and attention to grooming their long hair and luxuriant beards.

But in the Middle Ages hair does not seem to have received so much attention. Women often concealed it underneath a head–dress and hair on the forehead was plucked out so that they appeared to be bald. Men who had fought on the Crusades brought back the fashion for short hair, having found it easier to care for in a hot climate.

Left: In the Middle Ages a high forehead was considered beautiful
Right: Roman hairstyle

In Elizabethan times women's head-dresses went out of fashion and a lot of attention was focused on the hair. Both men and women cut it short because of the high ruffs they wore. They frizzed it with curling irons, padded it out, dyed it red-gold and coated it with a sort of brilliantine called pomatum which was made from a concoction of apple pressings mixed with hog's grease.

The most popular method of cleaning the hair was by using 'lye' which was a mixture of wood ash and water, but they only washed it 3 or 4 times a year. When the Queen lost her own hair she took to wearing wigs and this started a fashion for them.

A barber in Tudor times

By the 17th century, shoulder length hair was in fashion. Washing and caring for it was not easy with the soap and facilities they had then. Nits were common and they thrived in the long, badly washed hair. When Charles II re-introduced wigs, many men saw the advantages of wearing one. Apart from being in fashion, wearing a wig meant they could shave off their own hair and save themselves the trouble of caring for it. Samuel Pepys wrote in his diary:

'I did try 2 or 3 borders and periwigs, meaning to wear one; and yet I have no stomach for it, but that the pains of keeping my own hair clean is so great.'

The composer George Frederick Handel, wearing a full wig

Women like these had to sleep propped up, and washed their hair only twice a year. Hairdressers spent hours creating fantastic styles— though not quite so fantastic as the one on the right

A liniment to destroy Nits

Take Oil of Bays, Oil of Sweet Almonds, and old Hogs Lard, of each two ounces, powdered Stavesacre and Tansy Juice, of each half an ounce, the smaller Centaury and Salt of Sulphur, of each a drachm; mix the whole into a liniment. Before you use it, wash the hair with Vinegar.

The most grotesque and unhygienic hair-dos were worn in Georgian times, at the same time as the most grotesque make-up. During the 1770s and 1780s, women had their hair built up over wire foundations with great quantities of false hair added, until it reached fantastic heights. It was greased with pomatum and then had finely ground flour puffed on to it.

It was not possible to comb these hair styles. Once a week the 'head' had to be opened up to deal with the vermin which, attracted by the powder and pomatum, had become trapped inside. In between times, when the itching became unbearable, they probably inserted a little ivory hand on the end of a slender stick. This object was really designed as a back scratcher.

It is said that a gentleman called Lord Chesterfield, hearing someone remark that the ladies at Bath were wearing their hair 'three or four storeys high', replied 'Yes, and I believe every storey is inhabited, like the lodging houses here, for I observe a great deal of scratching.'

In Victorian times women and men continued to wear wigs and false pieces and to dye their hair or beards, though they tried to conceal the fact. Adverts spoke of preparations which 'restored hair to its natural colour' rather than dyeing it.

The Victorians continued to make hair pomades and conditioners at home, using recipes dating back to Elizabethan times. 'Lye' was still recommended as a shampoo and so were concoctions using egg. The most popular commercial dressing for men's hair was 'Rowland's Macassar Oil' which gave us the word anti-macassar for the cloths used on the backs of chairs to protect the upholstery from grease stains.

Young girls were taught to give their hair a hundred brush strokes a night to make it shine.

It was not until the early 20th century that hairdressing salons began to appear where women could go to have their hair washed and dressed by experts, instead of having to struggle with it at home. For those who still preferred to take care of their own hair, the task was made easier by the marketing of shampoos, setting lotions and dyes. People no longer had to mix their own.

False hair pieces were added to create a hair style

Hair salon, about 1940

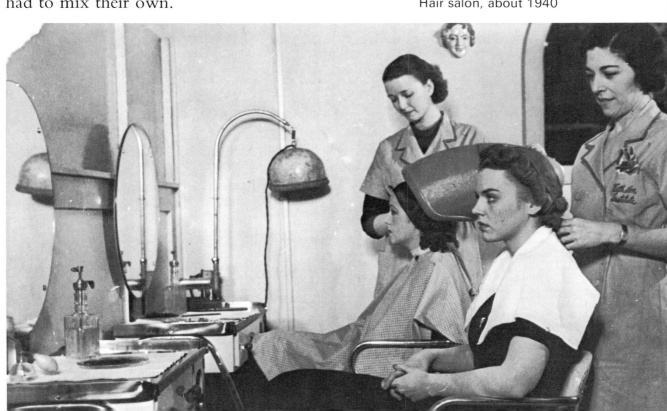

Teeth

Until recent times, people did not take much care of their teeth. The majority scarcely ever cleaned them, and when they did they used methods more likely to cause decay than prevent it.

Poorer folk often suffered from a disease called scurvy, caused by a lack of fruit and vegetables, which loosened their teeth and made their gums bleed. Filthy, rotting teeth, sore gums and foul breath were accepted as a fact of life—almost everybody over the age of twenty had them.

During the reign of Elizabeth I foreign visitors commented on the disgustingly bad state of English teeth. It was probably partly due to the Elizabethan fondness for eating sweetmeats such as marzipan. Even the Queen herself had yellow-coated teeth, which turned to jet black in her old age.

Tooth powders and tooth-picks

People did not really understand what caused tooth decay and bad smelling breath. When they concocted tooth powders for themselves at home they used such things as honey and sugar, crushed bones and fruit peel—even soot. To remove stains and discoloration, they used mixtures which included ground pumice stone, alabaster, brick and coral.

These mixtures certainly whitened the teeth, but they rotted or wore away the protective layer of enamel at the same time, hastening decay. A less harmful whitener was made of lemon juice mixed with burnt alum and salt.

Sometimes ready-made tooth powders were offered for sale.

Tooth powders were rubbed on with a tooth cloth made of coarse linen, often twisted round a stick. Afterwards the mouth was rinsed out with wine or sugary water. Some people also used tooth-picks. The rich had very elaborate ones made of gold or silver and decorated with jewels, but poorer people used bone or wooden ones. There is no evidence of a toothbrush being used in England until the middle of the 17th century. Until 1850 a toothbrush was considered quite a luxury.

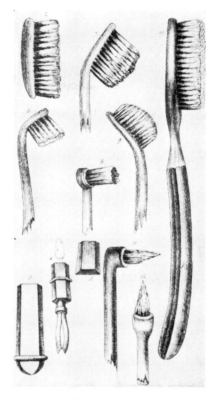

Early toothbrushes

One tooth powder claimed to 'whiten even the blackest teeth, preserve them from decay, cure toothache, fasten loose teeth and cure scurvy of the gums'

Two Ways to Whiten the Teeth

Dip a piece of clean rag in Vinegar of Squills, and rub the teeth and gums with it; it not only whitens, but softens and strengthens the roots of the teeth, and sweetens the breath.

Or

Rub the teeth well with Nettle or Tobacco Ashes, or rather with Vine Ashes and a little Honey.

Sometimes the victim had to be strapped down while his tooth was ripped out

People tried to disguise their foul-smelling breath with mouth-washes which they either bought or made at home. They were made up of ingredients such as wine, cinnamon, cloves, honey and orange peel. Sometimes people sucked perfumed pastilles.

Tooth drawers

Such poor care meant that most people suffered from toothache at times. But only when the pain became absolutely unbearable did they go to the surgeon-barber or 'tooth drawer' to have it out.

A visit to the tooth drawer was very different from a visit to the dentist. There was no adjustable dental chair and no anaesthetic. The troublesome tooth was ripped out of its socket with a pair of pliers or with a dreadful clawed instrument called a 'pelican'. No wonder patients sometimes had to be bound to the chair with leather straps!

Sometimes the operation was performed with the patient lying on the floor, his head gripped tight between the tooth drawer's knees. It is said that some people, driven mad by toothache, committed suicide rather than face the pain of having it out.

A live tooth is transplanted from the mouth of a poor man into that of a rich lady

Not all tooth drawers were skilled experts. Some quacks, wearing strings of teeth around their necks, travelled around the country performing the operation in the street or at fairs.

In Worcestershire in the 1880s and 90s a quack called Sequah was very well known. He dressed as a Sioux Indian chief, surrounded by Indian braves and a brass band. On one occasion he is said to have extracted 74 teeth in 57 minutes. As he drew a tooth he gave a nod to his band who roused their playing to such a terrific pitch that it drowned the yells of the patients!

Plumpers and transplantation

In the 18th century, fashionable ladies whose cheeks had sunken in due to the loss of teeth, put little balls of cork called 'plumpers' into their mouths to puff them out.

Those who had lost a front tooth sometimes filled the gap by having a tooth transplanted. This meant having a tooth from another person thrust into the socket. Such a high price was paid for a live tooth of the right size that poor people were willing to sell their good teeth to the rich. Teeth from the dead were also used. They were stolen from corpses rotting in graves and plundered from soldiers on battlefields.

False teeth

For a time human teeth were also used for making up sets of false teeth. After the great Battle of Waterloo in 1815 there was no shortage—many people had the teeth of dead soldiers in their mouths without knowing it.

Using second-hand teeth was not only rather gruesome, it was also unhygienic. There were no disinfectants in those days with which to treat the teeth. Sometimes they were boiled before being re-used, but not always. If the person from whom the tooth was taken had a disease, the person who received it was sometimes infected too.

False teeth makers of the 18th and early 19th centuries also experimented with teeth carved out of bone, ivory, or wood. One false tooth could be held in place by tying it to the adjoining teeth with gold wire, but this must have been very uncomfortable. A set of teeth to fill a larger gap caused even greater problems, for they had not discovered how to take an impression of the gums.

Even the most carefully made set would have fitted badly by our standards. Owners of false teeth had to be very careful not to laugh too heartily or talk too forcibly, otherwise they suffered the embarrassment of seeing their teeth flying across the room!

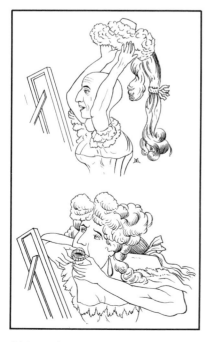

Aids to beauty

This extract from a letter written by a Mrs Purefoy in 1737 to 'Mr William Coryndon Operator for ye teeth' in London, shows that she is actually trying to get herself a set of false teeth by mail order:

'Mr Coryndon
I have sent you a bit of wood for a pattern the shape of which I believe will direct you. It must be made a little longer, the length of which I have sent you on a bit of tape. . . . I do believe the stick to be too thin at one end and too thick at t'other, but you must manage.'

Better fitting and cheaper false teeth did not appear until the late 19th century. By then dentists had started to use wax impressions and porcelain teeth set in rubber bases.

About the same time dentists also started to use anaesthetics and to experiment with cheaper methods of filling teeth instead of using gold which they had used in the past. People gradually became less afraid of visiting a dentist and mouths full of bad teeth, or toothless, sunken mouths became a rarer sight.

Jamieson's dental engine, 1886

Paris dental clinic, 1892

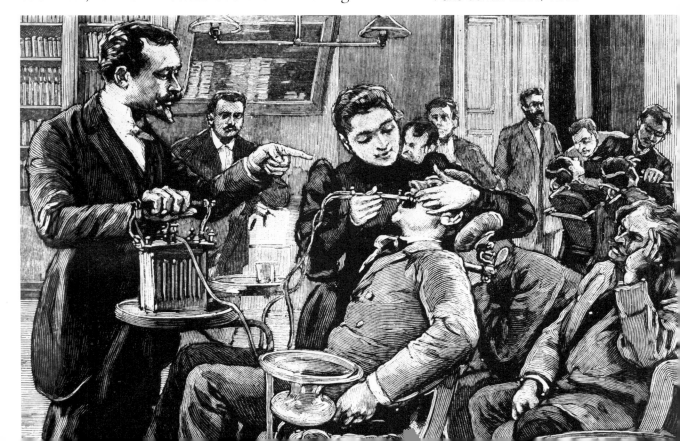

Women washing by a stream, beating clothes clean on wooden washboards

To take out Spots of Oil on Satin and other stuffs

If the spot is not of long standing, take the Ashes of sheeps trotters calcined, and apply them hot both under and upon the spot, lay thereon something heavy, and let it remain all night, and if in the morning the spot is not entirely effaced, renew the application repeatedly till the spot wholly disappears.

Washing clothes

Early times

In early times washing clothes was both difficult and unpleasant, for there were none of the things we now consider essential for washing—no hot water, no soap, no helpful gadgets, no machines to do the work.

Women had to carry the clothes in large baskets to a nearby stream where they soaked and washed them in the cold water. To loosen the dirt they had to pound the clothes with stones, or else paddle into the water and tread them with their bare feet, as many women in Asian and African countries still do.

Sometimes they smeared the clothes with mud or scoured them with dung to extract dirt. This was not so foolish as it sounds, for dung contains ammonia. When they had rinsed them, they spread the clothes on bushes or on the grass to dry.

Tudor times

Although people still preferred to do their washing out of doors, they were gradually starting to use their own yards and kitchens. Large houses were being built with a special stone-flagged room for laundry work. People now heated their water in big 'coppers' and used wash-tubs, specially bound with wooden hoops which would not rust-mark the clothes like iron ones.

Instead of beating out the dirt with stones, they spread the garments on a table and beat them vigorously with wooden bats or 'beetles'. Most households made their own washing soap, sometimes scenting it with herbs.

Plainer garments such as underwear were washed fairly frequently, yet often they were infested with lice. Boiling kills lice, but the fabrics of that time would not stand boiling. Presumably people learned to live with the torment, but there must have been a good deal of scratching.

When they put away the clean garments, Tudor housewives often placed sachets of perfumed powder amongst them. The most popular scent for this purpose was the violet-like scent of the orris-root.

Public washing grounds in Tudor times

Scottish girls by a burn, treading clothes in tubs to get out the dirt

No. 1362.
Goffering Irons.
10 ins. long, Polished Steel, Wood
Handles.
3 prongs, 2/2 each.   5 prongs, 2/8 each.

No. 1363.
Goffering Iron.
Nickelled Steel, Wood Handles.
3 prongs, 7/– doz.   5 prongs, 9/– doz.

To Clean Gold and Silver Lace

Take the Gall of an Ox and of
a Pike, mix them well
together in fair Water, and
rub the gold or silver with this
mixture, it will soon recover
its former lustre.

There were some rather strange and complicated
recipes for removing small stains, but none that would
remove perspiration stains from armpits. Tradition
had it that thistles would 'amend the rank smell of
armpits', but there were no deodorants or anti-
perspirants as we know them.

After a few wearings those heavy and elaborate
clothes must have stunk with sweat, especially if the
wearer had been doing something energetic such as
dancing or playing ball. Yet the fabrics from which
these clothes were made was very hard wearing and
often they were worn for years.

Because new clothes were costly they were even
passed on from generation to generation and it was
quite common for them to be bequeathed in wills.

Towards the end of the 16th century, ruffs became
fashionable for both men and women. Washing,
starching and crimping them involved a great deal of
extra work. The ruffs were crimped on a special sort
of iron called a goffering iron which was heated on
hot coals.

Wealthy Tudors wore magnificent gem-encrusted gowns,
delicate ruffs and fur-lined
doublets which were
impossible to wash

Eighteenth century

Washing methods had advanced very little, but household linen and clothes had increased in quantity. In small households the housewife tackled it a bit at a time with her daughters helping her, but in larger establishments the arrangements were more complicated.

It became the custom to let the washing accumulate for several weeks and then do the whole lot at one go. The servants were freed from their normal duties and washerwomen were employed to help them.

It usually took four days to complete all the washing and ironing. They worked from the crack of dawn, chopping sticks and filling coppers, rubbing and beating the clothes, and emptying tubs.

Sometimes the mistress used a washing tally which was an indicator showing how many tablecloths, sheets and other items had been put into the wash. She used it to check that all the items had been put back and that none had been stolen by the visiting washerwomen.

Women of the household got together to do the washing, ironing and mending

Dancing in a crowded ball-room was sweaty work

An elaborate dress like this was impossible to keep clean

It was the fashion in the 18th century as in Tudor times for the rich to dress themselves in outer garments made of sumptuous fabrics which were totally impractical to wash. Silk, satin, velvet, gold and silver brocade could not be washed without being spoilt.

The more fastidious rich passed on their clothes to servants once they were soiled and ordered new ones. Nevertheless, a gentleman of the times, Lord Hervey, wrote in his memoirs, 'At court last night, there was dice, dancing, crowding, sweating and stinking in abundance as usual', which suggests that even clothes worn at court must have lost their freshness very rapidly.

Sometimes perfumed sachets were sewn into the linings, but the fragrance did not last long and the odour of stale perfume must soon have mingled with the body odour.

Such were the difficulties involved in keeping clothes clean that we frequently hear of rich or celebrated people who did not particularly bother. Dr Johnson, one of the most famous figures of the 18th century, once confided to a friend that he had 'no passion for clean linen'—by which he meant clean shirts and underwear.

Cotton clothes and 'clean linen'

When raw cotton had to be imported from India and spun into cloth by hand, it was so expensive that few could afford to buy it. But when large quantities of raw cotton began to arrive from America and men such as Hargreaves and Kay invented machines which could spin and weave it into cloth, then cotton clothes became cheap and easy to buy.

By about 1800 people had begun to wear a fabric which was light and simple to wash and which, moreover, could be boiled clean of lice.

It became the fashion among the rich to wear scrupulously clean linen. A speck of snuff on a cuff or cravat was a source of shame to the wearer. This change was largely due to Beau Brummell who, you will remember, also insisted on bodily cleanliness. It is said that he sent his linen to be washed on Hampstead Heath and advised everybody else to do the same. He was so particular about having a clean apparel that he even had the soles of his boots polished!

FULL DRESS.

Light muslin was easy to wash

Clothes were still being washed by hand in the river in early 20th century, but this was unusual

Advertisement for washing soap

Washing soap

It was not until the second half of the 19th century that it was at last becoming easier for ordinary folk to wash their clothes. More and more households had running water laid on, or had access to a rain barrel. Also, when the tax was repealed in 1853 they could afford to buy slabs of yellow washing soap.

Soap firms, finding themselves with this vastly increasing market, began to experiment with different types of washing soap. As early as 1863 a soap powder called 'Hudson's Soap Extract' was introduced. By 1900 soapflakes had appeared. Firms ran big advertising campaigns for washing soap, as they did for toilet soap, in order to capture the new buyers.

Since the Second World War 'soapless detergents', made from mineral oils instead of animal and vegetable oils and fats, have become the type most popular for washing clothes.

Washday in 1910

Methods of doing the household wash had not improved much since the 18th century, but it had become a weekly routine.

Preparations started on a Saturday when the women of the household filled the copper with water and carried the dirty laundry down to the scullery in a big sheet to be sorted into separate piles of whites and coloureds, cottons and linens.

On Monday morning they made an early start. They lit a fire under the boiler using sticks and coal and put the first load in to boil.

Garments that were not boiled were washed in tubs made of galvanised metal, using a 'dolly' or 'posser' to force out the dirt. Very dirty clothes were scrubbed on a corrugated washboard. The housewife had to bend over the tub with her hands in the hot water, rubbing the clothes (and her knuckles) against the washboard's rough surface. It was a back-breaking job.

Laundry stove

The household wash. The woman on the left is using a posser or dolly in an old-fashioned wooden tub

This flat iron was heated by
burning methylated spirit

When they were clean, the heavy, wet clothes had to be lifted from the boiler or the wash-tub with a big stick and put into tubs of rinsing water. All the tubs had to be emptied by hand. Sometimes the rinsing water was 'blued' with a special powder to make the clothes look whiter. Starch had to be specially mixed.

Next the clothes were put through a big iron mangle with wooden rollers which pressed out the water. In large households they used a heavy box mangle which was weighted with stones.

Ironing day depended on when the clothes were dry. They ironed on the kitchen table, on top of a folded blanket covered by an old sheet. The most common irons were flat irons which had to be heated on the kitchen fire. Housewives spat on them and if the spit sizzled they were hot enough.

Washing methods like these continued in use until after the Second World War.

London slum-dwellers washing
clothes in the river

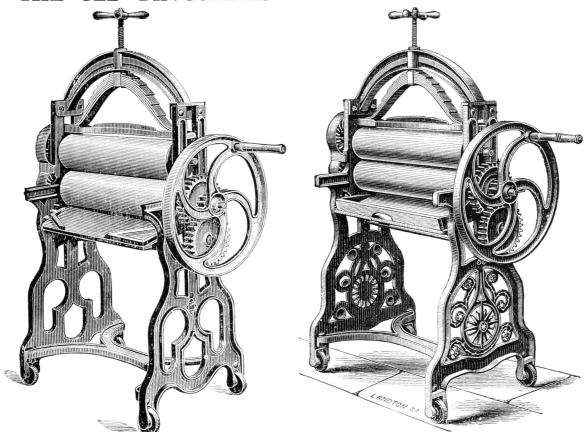

Public laundry, 1883

Early self-service launderette

Commercial laundries and dry-cleaning

Because of all the hard work and disruption caused by doing the household wash, it is hardly surprising that many people were prepared to pay a commercial laundry to take away their washing and do it for them. In the early days, even washing in commercial laundries was done by hand in tubs. It was a messy business and the staff sometimes wore rubber aprons and Wellington boots.

The discovery of dry-cleaning was a great advance. At last those garments made of fine or heavy fabrics could be cleaned without losing their new appearance.

The idea of dry-cleaning was introduced into England from Paris about 1860. It is said that the discovery that a spirit, such as benzine, could be used instead of water for cleaning clothes was made by accident. Some camphene, a fuel used for oil lamps, was spilled onto a gown. Instead of ruining it, the camphene was found to have cleaned it.

Washing machines

Washing machines did not start to become standard equipment in British kitchens until after the Second World War, even though some models were patented in the latter half of the 19th century.

America, Canada and Australia had experimented with them long before, because servants were not so easy to come by—with so many young immigrants looking for wives, girls could easily acquire a home of their own to work in. In Britain, maids, daily women and washerwomen were cheap to employ and fairly easy to find until after 1945.

The few early electric machines imported from Canada were too big and costly for the average British home. It was not until the 1950s, when smaller, cheaper models were marketed, that British families began buying them in large numbers.

Hand operated washing machine

Electric washing machines took much of the drudgery out of washday

An early electric washing machine

Nowadays, thanks to washing machines and driers and man-made fibres such as nylon and terylene, we can wash a garment, dry it and put it back on again within an hour. How different that is from the wash-days our ancestors knew!

But in the future children might well be horrified that we had to wash clothes at all. Already there have been experiments with paper clothes that can be thrown away after they have been worn once or twice.

Before we start congratulating ourselves on the cleanliness of our modern lives we ought to give a thought to the future. Even today, some foreign visitors are disgusted by the way the British soak in their own dirty water in a bath, instead of using a shower.

Fifty years from now, will people look back with amusement at such curious habits as submerging our bodies in hot water and rubbing them over with soap, or brushing our teeth twice a day with tooth paste? They might. . . .

Some other books

All these books were written for adults, but you might find them useful if you need further information.

Clean and Decent, the Fascinating History of the Bathroom and Water Closet Lawrence Wright (Routledge 1960).

The Strange Story of False Teeth John Woodforde (Routledge 1968 paperback by Tandem) and *The Strange Story of False Hair* John Woodforde (Routledge 1971). Both the last two have a clear text and some excellent illustrations.

Fashions in Make-Up Richard Corson (Peter Owen 1972). A long and detailed study of the history of make-up, with many recipes and illustrations.

A History of Make-Up Maggie Angeloglou (Studio Vista 1970). A shorter account than Richard Corson's book.

The Elizabethans at Home, The Jacobeans at Home, The Georgians at Home, The Early Victorians at Home, all by Elizabeth Burton (Secker & Warburg, paperback by Arrow). These contain information on hair, teeth, bathing, laundry and make-up.

'Lady at her toilette', by Aubrey Beardsley

Servants collecting water from a pump in the yard

Index